Shaking Hands with Tomorrow

An Independent School Leader's
Hard-Earned Lessons

Pete Jaques

To those generous and inspired teachers who make miracles.

Table of Contents

Introduction

A White-Haired Guy

One day a few summers ago after a lively meeting, I parted company with a dynamic Princeton Friends School mother. I walked across the ground Quakers have held since the late 1600s and up the stairs to my office in a 1781 schoolmaster's house. Then from my window I heard my meeting partner ask a young camp counselor if he had just seen "a white-haired guy" go into the building. She'd had an afterthought that couldn't wait, followed me until I disappeared, and didn't know where I'd gone. The counselor confirmed that such a guy had just gone inside, and up she came. Only later was I able to reflect on their easy description of me.

White, indeed, is what's left of my hair, and I've run my final career lap. Having been suddenly thrust into the position of middle school head in November of my first year of teaching, well before I knew enough to be there, I've since had the good luck to work in a number of schools that had real problems—as counterintuitive as that may seem. Not everyone gets the chance to experience so many agonizing challenges *and* be able to shape their solutions. As a long-time teacher, advisor, coach, department head, division head, occasional acting head of school, and trustee, I've had to be part of rethinking almost every aspect of independent school methodology—always intense, difficult, fun, and provocative. Those experiences forced me to learn for certain what does not work and what works best, often by trial and painful error. Along the way, I've evolved from smug preppy to egalitarian humanist, from miserable Episcopalian to agnostic to Quaker fellow traveler, and from unthinking traditionalist to committed progressive educator.

Much of what follows recounts what I've learned and what works, down to the details. Those matter a great deal. However, my overriding interest lies in the *outcomes* of schooling, and the details are what make better outcomes possible. I am moved to pass along some of what I have learned in my forty-nine-year career, to pay it forward. So I'm taking this stab at sharing with another generation of young committed school leaders a little hard-earned know-how. May it do some good.

September 2019, Vinalhaven, Maine

Chapter 1

The Parking Lot

7:28 a.m. on a raw November day. As I head out to the parking lot, I can hear the whistle on the Dinky, the little train that connects Princeton to the main track at Princeton Junction. Not good. This means there's an east wind, and my next forty-five minutes are going to be cold and damp. No matter—the first hug, the first smile, the first wry greeting by a middle schooler will warm things up.

A decade earlier, I had decided that Princeton Friends School needed a tamer parking lot and a better system for taking attendance so I chose to handle both by being there myself. It was among the best career decisions I'd ever made. Physically, it took only a clipboard, a huge baggie to cover it on rainy or snowy days, pencils in winter because ink freezes, and the right clothing; standing for forty-five minutes in one spot in a cold rain or prodigious winter wind required a little armor. On lovely spring and fall days, simply being surrounded by the trees and birds was worth it whether or not anyone showed up. Show up they did, of course; this was school. About half the students got out of their cars in the drop-off lane, and the others had parents who parked and walked in with them.

What happened in the next minute or two had weight all out of proportion to what transpired. You can learn a lot about children and families just by observing them arrive for school. After a few weeks, I could tell right away how things had started for almost every four-to fourteen-year-old, not to mention some of their parents and my colleagues. Some students popped out of their cars 100% ready to go, backpack in place and all squared away. Others had to stuff a week's worth of chaos back into the car before they could close the door, heap everything into their arms, and make their bedraggled ways to me across thirty feet of pavement.

More important, everyone shook my hand, and we shared morning greetings, sometimes reluctant, sometimes matter-of-fact, sometimes loving, and sometimes funny. It turned out that *my* morning mood was irrelevant; the first child invariably made me glad to be right there. Kids learned how to shake hands, of course—firm grip, eye contact, and words. Some four-year-olds took up to a year to ease into the shaking or eye contact or speaking, but eventually they all did. I learned a lot about parents too. Some were strangely controlling while others were restrained and simply watched their children be themselves; several became my friends through this shared morning ritual. Serial conversations unfolded in small chapters over days or weeks. I know I headed off a few hundred bad days out there, helping many an upset child to know that things would be OK despite the raised voices, the slammed door, or the misery that trailed out of their cars. Do you remember being, say, eight and heading into school that way? I used to have stomach aches until a grownup noticed and took the time to help me out. On some days in the parking lot, I was that adult. On others, I simply tipped off the right colleague. Both worked.

Most mornings, of course, almost everyone shook my hand, exchanged greetings of whatever sort the day brought, and went about their business. But the point—and the point of this book—had already been made before they hit the front door. Those children were not just showing up to attend classes and go home. They were whole people, if young ones, with all the needs that all of us have, and before they got to the front door they had been acknowledged, greeted individually, and cared about. What I was doing out there was modeling what works between people, and most would understand it later. I was shaking hands with tomorrow.

Having that impact in the parking lot is easy and often moving, if occasionally cold or wet. The greater trick is to make sure that what happens on the other side of the schoolhouse door is as responsive. That's what the rest of this book is about.

Chapter 2

Healthy Egos—
Our Most Important Product

At age 15 I started teaching tennis to 11-year-olds at a club, later taught baseball to local middle schoolers while at Harvard College, at age 22 began admitting high school students to Western Reserve University, and have since then worked almost entirely in education. In other words, I've been in the people business for 60 years. Presuming that I have acquired a little wisdom along the way, I submit that the single most important products of schools are healthy egos. Here is how I reached that unwavering conclusion.

I met and enjoyed some amazing people in my first job doing undergraduate admission at Western Reserve University (which after my first year merged with Case Institute of Technology). One remarkable 16-year-old invented the O-ring technology that made the Saturn rocket work. Another, a brilliant student, returned to Cleveland after a year of playing national-class Division I football for a Texas university that insisted he only take courses for knuckleheads. A third played the lead role in the *Lord of the Flies* movie. Meeting young people such as these but never really knowing them produced in me a growing dissatisfaction with admissions work. Subsequently, doing independent school fundraising at Milton Academy yielded the same frustration. So at Milton I began to work with 9th and 10th graders as an advisor and hockey coach around the edges of my development role. It was clear almost immediately that I was headed for a lifetime of teaching and working daily with young people, and thus I found my way to Moses Brown, an ancient Quaker school in Providence, Rhode Island.

Peter Mott, my forward-thinking former teacher and housemaster at Middlesex School and subsequent Moses Brown Head, hired me as a rookie middle school history teacher and two months later and utterly unexpectedly, installed me as middle school head following my predecessor's sudden and awkward departure. As a schoolboy, I had been pretty competent academically. Seldom, however, had I felt really engaged in what I was being taught, and typically I felt guilty about it, believing that the fault was my own. At Moses Brown, I saw young people following precisely in that path and needing what I had needed—more meaningful connection and personal engagement with their studies—but I just couldn't quite define it yet. At that point, my thinking and instincts were galvanized and buttressed by Douglas Heath, Professor of Psychology at Haverford College. I had too many children too young to have had either the time or the money to pursue a graduate degree, but both Moses Brown, as a Friends school, and the broader Quaker educational network made generous use of Dr. Heath at various conferences. What he had to say was like a shaft of bright light, inspiring me at precisely the point in my career at which I was questioning many aspects of the traditional, and purportedly excellent, education I had received at Shore Country Day School, Middlesex School, and Harvard College. (See his 1971 *Humanizing Schools: New Directions, New Decisions*, Hayden Book Company, Inc.)

In the mid-1970s, Dr. Heath was in his prime and a much sought-after speaker. For me to attempt to characterize his body of work would be presumptuous, but what he was doing early in his career was apparently groundbreaking in his field: he was looking at whole lives. His research involved following Haverford College men after they graduated. Very simply put, what I heard so clearly was this: *My research teaches that what adults need to be whole, fulfilled people definitely includes knowing how to be good colleagues, bosses, siblings, neigh-*

bors, spouses, parents, and citizens, as well as being trained in their fields of work. If those needs are so clear, why are we in schools only doing half the job, addressing only academic training?

The question riveted me and shaped my leadership from that point forward.

I do my best when I'm feeling confident. As a parent of six, I celebrated my children's successes and growth and watched them shrivel when they felt lousy about themselves. We've all seen that among students, of course. We educators, along with social workers and psychotherapists, know from our work with troubled youngsters and families that when things go wrong in young children's lives, their emotions need all kinds of unraveling, and they almost always feel badly about themselves. We've all seen bullying parents in public places like supermarkets denigrating their children for whatever their reasons. Those parents are the extreme examples, and when we know or read about their kids later in life, we watch them lash out too, repeating the cycle. I have learned that virtually every bully is, when the chain mail is peeled away, just a deeply wounded individual. On the other hand, I've known hundreds of despondent, stalled learners who have come to life with caring, effective attention from committed teachers in a positive environment. Based on these observations, I concluded long ago that people flourish only when they feel good about themselves and that most people who are flourishing become positive forces. Flourishing communities are built by flourishing people.

I have also reflected upon some of the unhappiest people I know. Many have had all the advantages American life has to offer, including a "great education." Yet despite their abundant talents, rich trappings, and even good grades, they are misery to be around for any length of time. To a man or woman, those people spent too much time in their young lives hearing that they were inadequate in some way, usually from their parents but too often from their schools as well. My most extreme examples are three former students who have been in prison, two of whom, Lyle and Erik Menendez, will be there for life, and yet they came out of one of the "best" independent schools in the United States.

Well-grounded, self-confident people have learned to be comfortable with the fact that life has its ups and downs, that their troubles are usually temporary and their gifts permanent, and that being successful usually involves finding and encouraging the best in others. Schools that consciously provide multiple, diverse, and evolving opportunities in which students can succeed are schools that promote such perspective and, along with their parents, teach young people how life beyond the classroom works. Decades of anecdotal evidence affirms my certainty that healthy egos are the key to emotionally healthy adult lives. We cannot wait for children to become young adults to *begin* teaching those lessons.

A few years after leaving Moses Brown for Princeton Day School, I became deeply involved with the Hyde School in Bath, Maine when one of my own children was in the midst of a couple of catastrophic teenage years. Joe Gauld was the founder and inspiration at Hyde. The title of his book sums up his principal point: *Character First: The Hyde School Difference.* Joe's school was organized around developing character; he believed that a student's academic training was irrelevant if his or her *life* was not working. As a result, Hyde's approach was distinctive: "if there's something wrong with the kid, there's something wrong with the family." Frank discussion of both students' and parents' attitudes and behavior were a priority, uncomfortably confrontational at times, and helped a lot of people deal with their accustomed hiding places. That tough-love program worked for hundreds of teens and parents, myself included.

Eventually, I came to see the work of Doug Heath and Joe Gauld as parallels. One of these distinguished educators was studying talented adults who had graduated from a selective, sought-after small college. The other worked exclusively with teens whose lives and families were a mess. Despite their widely disparate clienteles, Doug Heath's and Joe Gauld's messages were identical: *Whole lives matter.* I have been trying to build schools around that principle ever since.

Chapter 3

Students as Whole People

To my surprise, I learned early on at Moses Brown that teaching within a typical, traditional bell schedule was not the full antidote to the shallow relationships that had frustrated me in my admissions and development work. As a 9th grade advisor at Milton Academy, I sat through endless end-of-term faculty meetings, and was struck by how few of those teachers really knew their charges either as whole students or as whole people. When I began my teaching career at Moses Brown, the same was true, albeit in a smaller setting. As a teacher, I'd hear and observe my students' fractions of "air time" per class and correct their tests and read their papers, but that wasn't really knowing them unless I happened to work with them personally in some other way, such as tutoring or coaching. We teachers got a series of forty-minute snapshots of our kids, but a good look at the whole person was rare. Unless one was a student's advisor, how would one learn of Alice's serious work as an equestrian, Zoe's remarkable drawing ability, Henry's innate fairness and emotional maturity, Robert's deep political knowledge or Marita's advanced social conscience?

What I came to realize was that the *structure* of the school was keeping us from all of this wealth. More important, it was keeping children from having vastly fuller experiences, from more ways to shine and be recognized as shining by others. I began to understand a crucial sequence: That knowing each other precedes appreciation; that appreciation builds healthy egos; that healthy egos build flourishing people; and that flourishing people are secure enough to appreciate others, thus restarting the cycle. At Moses Brown, we teachers were nice people and were working very hard, but we were not fully able to initiate that sequence because we could not know our students well enough. Something was wrong.

It is certainly true that schools would not exist without academics. It is the training and the subsequent credentials for which most parents write tuition checks to independent schools. That's why we all use words such as *excellence* and *academic rigor* on our web pages and brochures. As academic training is our institutional core purpose, it is actually astonishing how little most individual teachers beyond elementary school really know about each of their learners. Early in my career, three distinct clues led to this realization.

The first clue appeared in faculty meetings held to discuss students. Thirty-five or so good people would be in the room, with some missing. (They were part-time or out coaching teams.) We would have an entire grade or a fixed number of kids to discuss. Each child would get a few of our collective minutes. Five or six teachers would comment. If the child was problematic, the discussion could go on for ten to twelve minutes (at the expense of time for others). Most of the teachers who did not teach that child would sit in silence, learning a little and perhaps contributing, but in fact not being too productive beyond surreptitiously grading a stack of quizzes. Even for the six or seven teachers of the specific child in question, those discussions were almost always a frustratingly shallow experience no matter how much we cared for those kids. We just didn't have enough time, and few of us knew many learners in depth. Sometimes we teachers came up with a consistent approach, but this was not easy to arrange and definitely harder to sustain. Despite the high quality of my fine and committed colleagues, such has been true in every traditionally bell-scheduled school in which I've worked over the past five decades.

The second clue came at report-writing time. A growing frustration early in my career was that I really could not *describe* students' learning because I didn't have a way to know each learner individually. And since faculty meetings were such unwieldy forums, I was frequently at a loss. Following up with individual colleagues depended on my zeal: I needed to go above and beyond just to do my job well, and that sometimes depended upon the luck of who was free during my free periods or who would tolerate regular evening phone calls. So, feeling inadequate at report-writing times, I would average up my marks, assign a term grade, and write a few sentences describing homework habits, attentiveness in class, and trends. But I was not in touch with my students' genuine learning. *Thin* was the word I used to describe my own reports, and I beat myself up three times a year every year for not being more zealous, even though I was a hardworking teacher.

A third clue appeared each May when we middle school teachers would meet with our lower school counterparts to learn what we had to know about each child so we could pick up where they left off. They operated in self-contained classrooms, but the structure changed to a traditional bell schedule at the 6th grade. I was always astonished and full of admiration and remorse over the differences between the extent of *their* knowledge of each child and ours.

Guided by my understanding of those experiences, it became clear to me that my middle school needed to change. We could not fully know our students as learners, and we seldom knew our children as whole people. There had to be a better way.

Chapter 4

Escaping the Bell Schedule

In a traditional bell schedule in a junior high or high school, administrators and department heads decide how many sections of each subject will be needed to accommodate the number of students in each grade or pair of grades. They then create a schedule that makes sense for the schedules of the faculty involved. Students are placed in these sections with little if any thought given to how their instruction or progress will be discussed. I believe it was this schedule, the standard for decades, that made it so difficult for teachers to talk meaningfully about how best to approach most students.

I arrived at Moses Brown at age 29 with seven years of non-academic administrative experience but I wanted most of all to be a history teacher. In November of my first year, when I suddenly became the Acting Head of Middle School, the word *clueless* certainly applied. In addition, the Middle School faculty as a whole was quite dysfunctional. There were great ranges in age, ability, energy, experience, teaching style, and alcohol intake, all unchecked by coherent pedagogical direction. We ran the gamut from stolid old-timers who knew their craft to exciting young, irreverent Vietnam-era "Turks" and a couple of nice folks whose futures obviously lay outside of teaching. But there was a good, committed core.

Once I gathered my wits and confidence enough to ask good questions, start conversations, and guide direction setting, we began to move toward the better way I mentioned above. In a fully collaborative process that included plenty of dissent, my colleagues were determined and not afraid to disagree. It took three full years, but we came to live with our differences and found a way to know students considerably better both as learners and as whole people. In the process, I was appreciative of and influenced by John Arnold, then Head of Middle School at Sidwell Friends, who had made a head start down the path we were following. More broadly, many of us were excited to be part of the national middle school revolution that was gathering steam. Realizing that 11- to 14-year-old students had considerably different needs than their older siblings, people such as us were questioning trapping them in junior high school schedules and approaches—thus, the "middle school" label was born. The challenge was to make the whole thing fit into the overall schedule and shared facilities of a PK-12 school.

Our solution was to divide our 180 students into three 6th–8th grade teams and assign four teachers to each: specialists in English, science, math, and history. They were charged with teaching those four subjects, being advisors, and creating micro-communities. The academic content had to agree across all three teams, but beyond that, each team was on its own.

Teams had their students from 8:15 until about 11, and from 1:30–3:15. In between, students had PE, art, music, shop, foreign language, and lunch. That took care of the requisite sharing of scarcer specialized facilities and single-subject teachers. Just as important, it allowed kids in the same grade to cross team lines and be with each other in, for example, 7th grade art, PE and French.

The new structure was an outright success. The four teachers came to know their sixty students intimately and could discuss them during the school day when the students were out at, say, woodshop or chorus. Their discussions provided better understanding of and more consistent approaches toward each student. That in turn accelerated each student's learning. Those improvements led to richer parent conferences and much more substantial written reports. Finally, each team created its own community time, and in those contexts, whole young people started to emerge. In one team, they launched an informal newspaper propelled by the brilliant cartoons of one boy. In another, jobs and micro-service emerged because kids wanted it. One team put on skits to wrap up each week—a novel form of review—and another started and ended each week in a community forum, beginning slowly, getting everyone on track together, and winding down calmly. In short, kids and teachers had chances to share their own gifts and to appreciate each others'. Finally, we made the decision to have students change teams for each of their three middle school years to avoid "better" or "worse" team labels and to keep everyone fresh. The professional growth implications for faculty members were profoundly positive and are enumerated in Chapter 6.

When I was leaving Moses Brown and interviewing for the Middle School Head position at Princeton Day School (PDS), I was asked point-blank if I was committed to the team concept, which seemed a little radical for that more conservative, better-established school. I replied that I was not wedded to the concept itself, but that I *was* committed to the principles that led to it: knowing learners better; knowing each child as a person; and finding ways for teachers to discuss them deeply and efficiently. That answer was good enough, and I was hired. After a couple of years, and after my excellent faculty had expressed all the usual frustrations with the traditional bell schedule, we launched the same conversations I'd had at Moses Brown. At PDS the outcome was core teaching groups. We subdivided each grade into two cores, being very careful not to make one "smart" and one "dumb," and assigned the smallest possible number of teachers to teach the same group of students. Key to it all, of course, was being certain that almost all of those teachers had at least one free period in common each week to discuss students. That accomplished, they had to keep excellent records so that the teachers who could not attend, e.g., the industrial arts faculty, would be informed and weigh in as well. It took close attention to communication, but the results were precisely the same as at Moses Brown: vastly improved knowledge of students, teaching, learning and reporting to parents.

Moses Brown's team structure began in 1975. It remains in place 44 years later because it is so effective. Thus, my point: traditional bell schedules impede teachers fully knowing and serving individual students as learners and as people. The far superior organizing principle is to *start* building school structures by matching small groups of teachers with small groups of students to ensure that those teachers can meet with each other weekly during the school day. It's that simple.

Chapter 5

Helping Kids to Shine

Once we structure a school wherein we really know children and teenagers, and they know one another, we can provide them with more chances to shine. All schools require the usual academic subjects and sports or PE classes, and most independent schools add technology, music, and visual and expressive arts as well. Lately, some of those courses have been reworked into STEM or STEAM offerings. But there's much more we can offer our charges—remember Doug Heath's message that we're helping to develop whole people, not just students. Independent schools are in a great position to do this because they have and can attract all sorts of different people—teachers, staff, and parents —who can offer all sorts of things without some of the structural impediments faced by public schools. Moreover, they are not paralyzed by teaching to state tests and thus can often spare a period a week.

The idea is that kids get to try things out, and some experiences stick. For example, Princeton Friends School (PFS) offered weekly lunch recess clubs in Spanish, chorus, global concerns, hand chimes, and folk dancing. The entire school from 1st to 8th grade sang together for fifteen to twenty minutes to wind up each week. For 3rd and up, PFS also devoted one period a week to "arts electives," relaxed activities for which students signed up in September for three seven-to-nine-week segments. In a school of 125 to 130 students, offerings have included coastal marine navigation, Indian cooking, circus arts, building model bridges, beading, jumping rope, chess, throwing a wiffle ball, hand chimes, knot tying, recorders, dramatic improv, filmmaking, cartooning, hip-hop, salsa, Chinese ribbon dancing, imagineering, bookbinding, basic woodworking, yarn balls, paper baskets, folk toys, jewelry, pillows, dolls, origami, mousetrap cars and other things that move. About ten were offered each trimester. Why? To broaden young people's horizons, provide a little know-how, add to their competencies, give them bragging rights as they move through their social worlds, and simply have fun. All that can happen in forty minutes per week.

At times other kids discovered a talent they admired greatly in someone on the periphery, and a whole new confidence emerged. A most compelling example occurred at Moses Brown. A 7th grade boy who had been a Cambodian boat person carried with him unspeakable horrors from that experience that the few of us in the know could only imagine. He had been adopted by a kindly family in Providence but at age 12 was starting every aspect of his life over, including an entirely new continent, new parents, new language, new culture, and new schooling, and he was socially disconnected and ever so lonely. He had nothing in common with anyone except a good mind, a great smile, and being 12 years old. However, there was a forty-foot-high climbing wall on one end of the field house built by a science teacher named Dave McNabb, and this boy tried it out. *Amazing* is where my description of his talent begins—the boy was a spider, fearless and able to do anything he wanted on that wall at great speed while the rest of us timorously made our way up, or just chickened out. Bingo! He garnered instant respect from cool kids and developed new friendships, and both endured. He was no longer alien.

That boy remains my single most iconic example of the power and importance of giving kids new and multiple opportunities to shine. In addition to traditional academic, athletic/kinesthetic, and artistic opportunities, independent schools can offer girls and boys a broad variety of new ways to feel good, admire one another, and build a more positive world.

Chapter 6

Faculty Hiring, Professional Growth, and Evaluation

Schools must be responsive places for adults as well as students if they are to sustain stability, retain and renew their best people, and consistently excel.

Starting with the best people makes doing so possible: Terrific teachers want to work with others of their ilk. Conversely, coping with the outcomes of hiring weak ones is wearing and discouraging and can prompt strong colleagues to move on. I've seen that too often: students or parents coming to trusted teachers in frustration because a weak colleague doesn't return papers on time, holds disorganized classes, can't control students, plays favorites, and so forth; advisors coming to administrators to report all of those issues or because the teacher in question is frequently late to meetings, doesn't follow lesson plans, doesn't return phone calls and emails, and the like. There is real value in hiring with great care and getting it right the first time.

➢ Spend time with key departmental or grade level colleagues and administrators to talk through what's wanted, in all its nuances, before developing a profile that will become an online job posting.

- ➤ In addition to posting positions, get word out through parents and faculty; they share a vested interest in successful searches and they often know of good teachers and staff members in other communities who may be looking.
- ➤ Establish systems for acknowledging responses to listings or unsolicited inquiries. Prompt well-worded acknowledgments are impressive, while sloppiness and silence are not. It is important to write promptly to those who are not a good fit, telling them why and complimenting what you can.
- ➤ After the great sorting, conduct phone or FaceTime interviews, but first develop a standard matrix for those calls to help with accurate recall later.
- ➤ Provide in-person interviewees fair notice about what to wear and the time frame involved.
- ➤ Since a teacher who writes poorly will be a permanent burden, give each candidate a ten-minute handwritten assignment to be done at school.
- ➤ Discuss the details of one best practice as a means to assess depth.
- ➤ Check references with great care.

Once a school has hired strong colleagues, motivating and retaining them is what attracts the best new students, families, trustees, donors, and public recognition. Insisting upon professional growth is a key to such prosperity for two principal reasons. First, teachers and administrators are innately prone to burnout. That derives from doing essentially the same thing year after year for decades with little inherent structural opportunity for significant change. Second, teachers work many hours a day alone with children, work hard and have overwhelming reasons to keep focused on the details. Losing breadth of vision simply comes with that territory. The sense of staleness that edges in over time for so many is the beginning of burnout. Left unchecked, it grows. Students, parents, colleagues, and the school's reputation lose once it becomes clear that a formerly vibrant faculty member has started going through the motions. The tendency for this to happen is a widespread, nationally recognized occupational hazard, and smart boards and leaders understand these realities and build in opportunities for, and insistence upon, significant growth.

There are many ways to grow professionally. There is no substitute for extensive training in a specific area, such as a graduate degree in one's field or programmatic training, e.g., the Wilson Method for reading specialists or Junior Great Books for teachers of literature. Other coursework, seminars, workshops, and in-service training all have their places. Some fortunate schools still provide sabbaticals or summer travel grants. Many insist that teachers visit another school or take a day to observe classes within their school once or twice a year. These are all widely accepted, tried-and-true stimulants. However, my experience is that for fully employed teachers, such solutions often amount to islands in a stream—nice moments of respite and reflection that are quickly left behind once they are re-immersed in their always-too-hurried daily lives. For that reason, I believe the two most productive forms of professional development are ongoing, frequent conversation during the school day with a small group of colleagues about children taught in common and a good evaluation-for-growth system.

In a previous chapter, I described the three middle school teams at Moses Brown School and the core teaching groups at Princeton Day School. In each of those, the introduction of the new structure exponentially improved the quality of teachers' discussions about children. Unlike the conversations in most large after-school faculty meetings, those in teams and cores kept everyone involved because the teachers all taught the same young people and every conversation mattered. In addition, teachers learned so much more from one another: Newer teachers sat at the feet of the more experienced; those better at being advisors inadvertently or explicitly provided how-to advice; the individual who "got" that one opaque child or parent taught others what worked; experienced new teachers brought ideas from other schools; and everyone shared resources and tricks of the trade. People came to know and trust each other by working together so intimately and could be more open about their individual concerns or weak suits, be receptive to practical advice and observations, and consciously improve their professional practices in supportive environs. Everyone came to know his or her students better, provided improved approaches to them, and were proud of it. In short, the meetings to discuss children amounted to powerful weekly professional growth experiences for thirty-three weeks a year plus summer.

Even with such positive day-to-day experiences, individual programs of reinvigoration and career renewal are needed. Those can only come from periodic, substantial, personal evaluations. Faculty evaluation is a loaded topic. It can frighten many teachers. Business people employ and expect annual evaluations as a matter of course, but business models don't translate well to independent school teaching. The recurring national debate over merit-based pay for teachers always involves evaluating performance, but how to measure performance is the heart of the conflict and passionately disputed.

Trustees and accrediting groups correctly insist that schools have an evaluation system in place for teachers and administrators. In my experience, there is absolutely no way to meaningfully evaluate every teacher and administrator every year. There simply is not time for a head, dean, or division head to do the job well and when attempted, the end product is too shallow to be worth it. In addition, people in different professional and personal circumstances need different kinds of evaluations. Finally, it is clear that if a possible outcome of an evaluation is losing one's job, the individual being evaluated has no motivation to admit a weakness or ask for help with a particular issue.

Recognizing all of these realities and frustrations, a committee I chaired at Princeton Day School in the early 1980s set out to create something new and better. It took many months and much convincing, but we succeeded in developing four powerful principles.

A. Both rookie teachers and those in their first year at a school begin in an openly probationary track, one with frequent observations and conversations designed to be supportive, all leading to a decision in January of that first year about whether or not returning is appropriate.

B. Teachers whose contract renewal is in question are formally placed in a separate track with clear written statements from the head of school describing the problems, desired solutions, supports, evaluators, and deadlines. If an individual has not been officially notified of placement in this track, losing his or her job in the main evaluation-for-growth track is entirely off the table.

C. Teachers and administrators whose contract renewal is not in question nonetheless need evaluations for growth. With potential loss of job out of the question and complete confidentially emphasized, they will be more inclined to be open with their evaluators. They do not need to waste their time on shallow annual reviews because they do their jobs competently and even brilliantly. To permit meaningful depth of process, their full evaluations should occur only once every three to four years, with just one-third or one-quarter of the faculty in the process each year.

D. Always launch an evaluation for growth with a full self-assessment. Ours specified (1) a description of the teacher's or administrator's career path to date; (2) a detailed recitation of current responsibilities and how she or he felt about each one; (3) projected and desired next career step(s); and (4) a focusing question or a request for specific guidance.

It was heartening to see these four principles reaffirmed by no less an expert than Charlotte Danielson in her article in *Education Week* of April 18, 2016, thirty-five years after our committee's work at PDS. While the principles stood the test of time, the system we set up was initially too labor-intensive and needed streamlining. Such structures can vary, but in order to ensure professional growth and satisfy the requirement of trustees and accreditors for verifiable evaluation, a system of accountability has to be built in. Assuming an evaluation for growth every three or four years that includes specific recommendations, portions of the recommendations should be set as annual goals.

A supervisor should oversee and record progress toward them, and that progress should be reported in the next major self-evaluation.

The rewards of such a system are potent:

> - Teachers and administrators avoid burnout by growing.
> - Turnover among strong people is reduced; thus, excellence is sustained.
> - A higher level of professionalism encourages reciprocal growth across staff.
> - Trustees and accrediting agencies know that annual monitoring keeps people accountable.
> - Students clearly benefit.
> - Positive word-of-mouth reports enhance recruiting, admission and development efforts.

Experience provides some practical lessons for conducting these substantial evaluations:

> - Give six month's notice of a self-assessment's due date, and allow two weeks for it to be read and considered.
> - Allow two hours for scheduling observations and interviews, and budget funds to pay substitutes.
> - To sustain momentum, allow one month for gathering information and compiling responses.
> - Meet off campus for a half-day to deliver the findings, which are guaranteed to be celebratory and deeply felt by all.
> - At the conclusion, destroy self-assessments and every physical and digital note. Give copies of the final report only to the head of school, the person being evaluated, and whomever will guide subsequent work on the recommendations.

Beyond ensuring personal safety, there is nothing more important to which a school should devote its resources than effective hiring and evaluation-for-growth practices.

Chapter 7

Firm Leadership vs. Conflict Aversion

Human frailty has been on full display of late. Given its scope, the Catholic Church is the clear leader in the abuse of children and in covering it up. In this digital information age, we in schools know that our adult population is hardly immune as more and more schools go public with apologetic revelations. A tiny percentage of adults in charge of children always find ways to abuse them sexually. I don't believe there is any difference between the bishops and cardinals who have been hiding and transferring pedophiles and the heads of schools who do not take all the steps necessary to identify perpetrators and inform police and other schools about them. Heads may have had many motivations to avoid doing so: the "boys will be boys" mindset; the accused having been their friends for years; not wanting to publicly embarrass the perpetrators' families; or a reluctance to "air the school's dirty laundry" lest doing so negatively impact admission and development. At this point, the proverbial chickens have come home to roost for far too many schools in the form of vast personal and institutional embarrassment, tarnished legacies, enormous legal fees, insurance premiums and financial settlements, and unanticipated negative effects upon admission and development yields.

We now know that the impacts on victims of sexual abuse and romantic approaches can be debilitating for decades or for life. Such acts by adults *including covering them up* are both unconscionable and illegal. To my mind, the *one* deterrent that has a chance of working is making it known that, if exposed, a sexual abuser of children and adolescents and anyone who traffics in child pornography *legally must, and automatically will, be reported to police, as well as suspended or fired immediately.* Heads of schools and boards of trustees must make clear that *every* school response to sexual/romantic/pornographic predation will absolutely involve the criminal justice system.

Being filled with agreeable people and the hopeful power of youth, independent schools are inherently pleasant places to work. However, a lot of us are so nice as to be conflict-averse. Too rare are the administrators who act decisively and promptly when it is clear that a faculty or staff member's situation is irretrievable. Instead, they too often counsel gently and permit someone to stay for years after it's clear he or she should not have had a contract renewed. A teacher who cannot command respect, interest students, or enforce rules and standards must be let go. Inaction by the head of school is always unfair to the students directly involved, their tuition-paying parents, the colleagues who are undermined in their own adherence to standards, and the admission and development directors whose success depends in large part on the perception of the school as a responsive, competent place. Ultimately, the head's credibility is imperiled. Heads must learn to keep paper trails and act. Strong hiring and brave pruning are among the most important things a head does to sustain a school.

"Don't smile 'til Christmas" was once advice given to rookie teachers on how to garner respect from students. It was extreme but contained seeds of truth. Its opposite is teachers who try to curry friendships and popularity with students. Doing so is a sure path to losing their respect and thus the ability to draw clear, firm lines and be effective. Jeannie Norris, long-time head of Miss Hall's School, annually advised her faculty that, "Students don't need teachers to be their friends. They have friends. They need us to be friendly." One successful rookie performer was David Lightfoot at The Pennington School. As a new middle school teacher in a 6th-12th grade school, he was fearless about correcting the behavior of even the oldest students whose names he had not yet learned. When I complimented him, he said, "If I walk past it once, it will just be harder to fix the next time." At first he was not popular, but he surely earned everyone's respect, became an effective faculty member whom the students admired, and was appointed in due course to a leadership position. Conversely, I have known too many new teachers who spent their first terms or years being the coolest and most fun for students. After a period of infatuation, most students inevitably saw through the routine; the loss of respect was irretrievable in many cases, and, if not, it took at least two years to build a new image.

I have been guilty of being slow to rein in such false gods. It is not just to rescue them that we administrators must step in early. My experience is that every minute devoted to yet another cool story is one in which something more valuable goes unlearned. Further, the bedazzling light of these shooting stars too often casts the rest of us in an unflattering and undeserved shadow and can be a source of resentment. The best students and teachers usually see through it immediately but are effectively powerless. In other words, students and colleagues need a leader's protection. My advice is to step in early and firmly at the first whiff of such narcissism. Providing specific case-study advice during new faculty orientations can help.

Chapter 8

Meetings That Work

Meetings are crucial. Consistently good ones can lift a whole school. Bad ones are expensive and corrosive. Many Quaker and other schools make most decisions by a consensus-like "sense of the meeting" (actually a highly developed art form) while others opt for greater efficiency. Yet in schools of all sorts, meetings can be deadly, far too long, and unproductive. When the people scheduled to attend the next meeting dread going, the institution is being eroded.

Miserable meetings have driven many to find better ways. I thank all those colleagues who have discovered and shared methods to make meetings productive, interesting and even vibrant. Here are a dozen procedures that work:

1. Cancel meetings when possible. Do not have people attend who will be wasting most of their time. Expect them only at the right portion of the meeting and manage meeting time around them.
2. Know that there are different kinds of meetings. The key to success is being clear on what kind suits each situation and being disciplined within them.
3. Have an agenda for every meeting, disseminate it to all attendees via e-mail at least 24 hours in advance, and post it visibly at the meeting itself.

4. Leave time in every meeting to introduce new concerns even though they might be deferred. Maintain a public running list of topics that have been sidelined; it prevents them from being lost and honors those people who brought them forward. The bottoms of agendas are one good place for this.

5. Know in advance who will lead and close the meeting. He or she should strive to be prepared.

6. Set starting times realistically, allowing people time to visit a restroom, make a quick phone call or e-mail, or grab a cup of tea. Then insist on starting promptly. As one who is prompt, I am resentful of those who consistently waste five or ten minutes of my time by being late. Life does intervene for each of us at times, but not *usually*.

7. Start with 90 seconds of silence in the manner of Quakers. It does wonders for focus and mutual appreciation.

8. Keep excellent notes at every meeting. I've been in too many meetings after which people could not agree on what was decided only a week before. Publish notes promptly via e-mail if the school's network is secure. Never send them to home addresses. Identify action steps and their due dates.

9. Start the next meeting with a review of progress on those action steps. Doing so promotes a culture of effectiveness.

10. Know in advance what will be announced at meetings and strive to have those items included with the agenda to conserve meeting time.

11. Know in advance what parts of each meeting will require discussion, and publish how the matter(s) will be decided. Sometimes the leader will only gather information and opinions and will make a decision unilaterally. At other times and on significant decisions, it is important to hear everyone's voice; if a few people pass to ponder in the first round, be sure to get back to them before moving ahead.

12. Some topics are going to be huge, e.g., revising the faculty evaluation system or the schedule. In such cases, there is risk of endless discussion. One successful streamlining device is to

designate a working group to carry the job forward. The head of school, after due consultations, appoints the chair of the working group, announces the calendar, and invites individuals to join. In the initial meeting(s) on the topic, the full faculty and staff can share their thoughts while the chair takes careful notes. The working group is then charged with returning on the specified date to present its findings and recommendations. It's best if the group's roster does not exceed single digits in number, but it is more important that any interested party is able to volunteer for membership. Benefits: Everyone's voice is heard in the opening meetings; subsequent meetings are streamlined by working in a smaller group (which can always reach out to specific individuals as needed); members of that working group have a professional growth experience (it's a great place to bring along young teachers); all angles are considered and acknowledged during the final presentation; and the work gets done with considerable efficiency.

There are three keys to success: (1) the head or division head appointing the working group's leader wisely (2) setting aside time for the group's meetings and (3) managing responses to the final presentation of findings. Michael Zimmerman, my successor as Head of School at Friends School Haverford, taught that after such a working group's final presentation to the whole faculty, everyone again gets to respond, but *only* to ask clarifying questions and then approve or disapprove, not to make suggestions: If someone wanted to be in on the discussion following the opening meeting(s), he or she would have to have joined the group at the outset. It's an effective model because everyone has a chance to weigh in, but conclusions are reached and matters move forward.

Twins at their older sister's Princeton Friends School graduation.
Photo by Sue Jaques

I shook hands daily with every Princeton Friends School student and colleague.
Photo by Sarah Crossman

*Introducing Punahou School kindergarteners to
the unknown woodchuck.*
Photo by Sue Jaques

*A happy moment after leading a Princeton Day
School graduation.*
Photo from Princeton Day School Archives

Organizing groups at an assembly at Princeton Friends School.
Photo by Chrissie Knight

Indian Folktales literature class thanking a friend for her slides of India.
Photo by Chrissie Knight

Fourth grade medieval fletchers showing off their new arrows.
Photo by Dave Gibson

A friendly Red Sox-Yankees rivalry.
Photo by Chrissie Knight

Chapter 9

Discipline That Succeeds

When facing student behavioral issues, both absolutely rigid and bleeding-heart school cultures have driven me nuts. The former is exemplified by "zero tolerance" policies found in many public school districts and some independent high schools. Extreme examples include the nonsensical lengthy "sexual harassment" suspensions of four- or five- year-olds for touching a classmate in the wrong place and the automatic expulsions of promising young adults for momentary and developmentally predictable lapses in judgment. Common sense and common humanity get lost under such policies. Conversely, bleeding-heart responses to students who obviously need clear boundaries hurt everyone. Miscreants don't change their behaviors and as a result they undermine respect and credibility. They also create resentment and resignation among the vast majority of students and teachers who are doing things right. Thus, the middle ground is the best, albeit more complex, place to be.

Every effective disciplinary system needs (a) simple, clear communication and (b) three levels of responses to students.

Clear Communication

1. Write and publish the rules, simplified into categories. All schools do this.

2. Write and publish the predictable school response to each level and frequency of infraction. Most schools do this, too.

3. Train the faculty on the *spirit* and *intention* of operating the system in your school. In my schools, we have emphasized talking students out of typical minor misbehaviors up to a point beyond which lies bleeding-heart territory. Get clear on your spirit and intentions so you can train everyone to respond consistently.

4. Virtually every independent school gives each student an advisor, and advisors are charged with knowing everything that is going on with each advisee. Therefore, advisors must be informed about their advisees' disciplinary matters.

5. However, since advisors are also charged with being each advisee's champion, they cannot be the prosecutors as well. They may agree with disciplinary action but always from a supportive point of view. This is important. Therefore, each school needs an administrator to manage the disciplinary system, which has the additional benefit of promoting consistency.

6. A chronic problem for overly busy teachers is how to communicate about minor behavioral issues. Below is a form that does the trick, takes little time to complete, makes it clear which adult is doing what, and allows an adult to express frustration privately while permitting the system to provide a more measured response. If young Xavier is having a terrible day, for example, and teachers use the simple form promptly, his advisor and the administrator will know it quickly and can choose how to respond because copies of the form will have gone to them.

7. My experience is that a paper form on a pad is simpler and more likely to be completed promptly than if requiring digital log-in, but either way, documenting minor issues is important *and will remain important weeks and months later* when reviewing patterns of behavior and conferring with parents.

Student _____

Teacher _____ Date _____

What behavior prompted this slip?

❑ Lateness to class
❑ Excessive talking
❑ Disrespect for property _____
❑ Gum chewing, candy, etc.
❑ Inappropriate use of electronic devices _____
❑ Rudeness/inappropriate language
❑ Wrong place/wrong time
❑ Running indoors/endangering others
❑ Other or details: _____

Behavior is: ❑ Recent   ❑ Chronic

Action:

❑ Just FYI—I'm handling the incident
❑ Please confer with me
❑ More info attached
❑ Other: _____

Please give **original** to student's advisor: _____
Please give **copy** to student's division coordinator.

Three Levels of Disciplinary Responses

Level 1 – Talk students into eliminating disruptive behaviors and talk more urgently about minor infractions against property and people. My experience is that 97% of problems can be persuaded away. *But regardless, record the minor incidents on those forms so that progress or lack of it can be recalled later*, and advisors will know what is happening in the moment; checking the box for "I am handling this with the student" does the trick.

Level 2 – Install some kind of detention system; it is the only way to avoid having the same conversation with the same student about the same issue ad nauseam and not jump to major disciplinary action. It is the "enough is enough!" response after persuasion hasn't worked. The trick is to make the detention just painful enough to get student and parental attention. Nuances are:

> ➤ The reporting teacher can recommend a detention, but the advisor must agree. This is a useful safety valve in cases of a misunderstanding or the reporting teacher having a bad day. Mutual professional respect eliminates undermining, and an advisor–teacher chat can quickly discern the best path.
> ➤ The school predetermines two after-school detention times per week so detentions can be served promptly. The administrator informs the parent of the assigned afternoon, working around things like long-scheduled medical or dental appointments. The detention supersedes any school rehearsal, athletic practice or game, or club meeting.
> ➤ During the detention, the student may only sit upright and think and may not read, do work, listen to music, use an electronic device, or sleep. At Princeton Friends, we called detention an "Opportunity for Reflection" and built in a short counseling conversation about the problem and possible solution during the 45-minute period. Students still called it a detention, but they did reflect.

Level 3 – Major disciplinary responses can and should be quite nuanced. Parents, of course, must always be consulted before the final verdict is handed down. Except for intolerably shocking, hostile acts that require stunning suspensions or immediate permanent removal from the community, responses should be individually tiered to avoid the rigidity of broader "zero tolerance" policies. I have had excellent success using probation as a first major disciplinary step.

Probation works well for middle and high schoolers for whom detentions are not a sufficient deterrent, who persist in chronic minor misbehavior (which is frustrating for everyone), and who just need to learn that the school is serious. Violation of a probation's terms must end in suspension or worse. Therefore, clear definitions matter, and probation is best served when it is narrowly defined and long enough to firm up changing behavior. If for example the precipitating behavior is disruptiveness in class, a student should not be considered in violation and suspended for an unrelated matter such as chronic lateness or disrespect of property. My experience is that probations should last two to three months for middle and high school students. They should start with official letters that clearly define terms and length and that are handed to the student in the presence of advisor and parent, with copies to advisor, parent, and file. Such letters should emphasize that the student is in charge of the outcome: violation means automatic suspension, which goes on the record, while no violation means that the lesson has been learned and the matter is closed. The latter, of course, is the objective. At probation's end, the student should receive a second letter stating that it is over and applauding its successful completion, with copies distributed as above.

Suspension is another tool that can be used in a nuanced way. At the lower elementary level it replaces probation, which is too subtle for most youngsters to grasp. It usually lasts an afternoon or a day. It reassures those who were victimized by some unacceptable behavior, and it makes the requisite point to the offending child and parents. At the middle school level and beyond, suspension is a graver matter as it is the step before expulsion. It is either a good response to a violation of probation or a first response to a violation of a major school rule. In both cases, it teaches. Followed by probation, it sends a strong message and still allows room for the perpetrator to learn the lesson and get on with his or her life without bearing the stigma of expulsion.

Expulsion, as differentiated from the counseling out of a student whose issues are beyond the school's capacities, always represents failure on the part of the student, the parents, and the school. Yet it often has a positive outcome. Of the dozen or so kids I have "kicked out" in my time, most have thanked me years later for waking them up and, in some cases, for turning their lives around. As professionals, we never stop learning or being surprised.

Chapter 10

Parents—Community and Respect

School parents entrust us with their children and, to some extent, their children's futures. They pay our salaries and benefits, are generous with their time, expertise, contacts, and donations, attract new friends and families to the school, and sometimes become our own good friends. Yet in some schools, they are collectively and instinctively regarded warily, if not flat-out defensively. That's foolish.

Before professing to know something about the subject of our students' parents, I must acknowledge that the independent school world is pretty fortunate. We have admissions offices and can admit whom we choose. Thus, we don't have to deal too often with the uncaring, the completely inattentive, the unbalanced or the careworn desperate parents of students with profound personal, medical, and cognitive problems. I have always admired my public school counterparts who manage such extremes daily. On the other hand, independent school parents get to vote with their feet by abandoning schools that are doing a lousy job, as school closures attest. So while we may start on an easier path than our public school counterparts, our very existence depends upon our performance.

My career has included two short stints in the profit-making world, one in corporate outplacement, the other in the contracting business. Those two experiences taught me to respect the people who earn enough money to pay independent school tuitions, which is difficult to do in our current economic climate. In my younger days, I worked with a number of colleagues who could be quite critical of some parents. Several of the critics were single or childless. I admit to having joined in at times, even though I had children of my own. Some of our targets were deserving, but looking back, I wince at our collective arrogance or ignorance—our lives had been relatively unblemished by hardship. Fortunately, my early hubris was gradually erased by multiple people: the mother who knew vastly more about her child's learning difference than any of us and embarrassed me into a crash course in dyslexia; the father who as my volunteer assistant football coach gave me needed perspective on 15-year-olds one day when I had misplaced mine; the parent association leaders who pressed me to do a better job of feeding their children good food until they succeeded; and the single mother who turned out to be mentally ill and needed our help, not our self-righteousness. The last of my callousness was finished off by training from therapists in both professional and personal contexts, and by raising six teenagers, one of whom suffered from a mental illness. A colleague at Princeton Friends, Bonnie Benbow, taught me to always presume that parents were doing the best they could. Simply recalling that wisdom has helped me begin numerous conversations on a more positive basis.

Here is a set of sequential truths about parents. School may occupy most of students' days but it is only a part of their life upbringing. Family is primary. We may think we know better than parents do, but experience teaches that what we think can be wrong or irrelevant. We may not understand or agree with a family's values or methods, but unless we believe a child is genuinely endangered, we must honor them. Schooling is most effective when parents and teachers are partners—an intention all schools claim. To be genuine partners, we must be open to understanding each family. Trust and understanding come from knowing one another. If we bump into each other frequently, we learn one another's names and become familiar enough so that important conversations about children don't have to start between strangers. All this being said, schools must create genuinely welcoming atmospheres, and that requires faith in positive outcomes, often beginning with simple, consistent smiles.

Having suffered in schools in which the relationship with parents was frequently or even chronically toxic, I attest to the importance of very conscious community building. That said, schools must establish and maintain boundaries and procedures to ensure professionalism and protect faculty members from parents who may be over-reactive, over-controlling, always want to start with a senior administrator, or are just used to having things their way. Some basics:

1. Whichever school leader hears a concern or complaint first must not become the first responder unless there is a true crisis. Doing so minimizes teachers and advisors, slows their professional growth, and encourages further "end runs."

2. Heads or division heads should insist that a parent with a concern or complaint about a teacher or incident see that teacher first, and then should quickly inform the teacher to expect that contact soon. The wise teacher will immediately initiate the conversation.

3. Heads or division heads should insist that the parent see the advisor first for a broader picture of a child's educational or social experience, since at most schools, the advisor is set up as the hub of such knowledge.

4. However, if the issue is a repeated complaint about an individual teacher or advisor, a concerned parent should approach the division head first, and so forth up the line.

A most corrosive factor in faculty morale is a head of school or division head who, upon hearing a parental complaint, consistently sides with the complainer. Furthermore, boards of trustees that hire heads of school who have not done time in the academic trenches as division heads are taking a considerable risk: The uncertainty or insecurity of those heads when the chips are down with a problematic student, teacher, parent or trustee can cause real damage. Conversely, a faculty that is treated respectfully and professionally is likely to take pride in acting professionally and will grow better at it.

Clear and prompt internal communication usually solves most problems born of misunderstandings. Keeping advisors informed of minor student issues with overdue work or misbehavior helps an advisor see the total picture of a child. A quick clarifying chat between advisor and reporting teacher ensures that everyone is in the loop. Furthermore, a teacher or advisor taking a moment to send a brief voicemail, text or email to the division head to report a significant incident puts that administrator in a position to respond calmly when others inquire or the rumor mill is abuzz. The same applies for a head of school.

It is also important to allow leaders and teachers room to get things wrong. For example, any one of us can interpret a student social situation incorrectly, jump to an inaccurate conclusion, speak more firmly than we should under the circumstances, or just be grumpy—we all have our moments. In a mutually supportive professional culture, an advisor can support a child who is reporting an unfair action by a teacher and undo a misunderstanding and clear things up before the end of the day. That kind of climate builds student and parental trust.

Written Progress Reports

Reporting to parents on student progress can be made more problem-proof by following some proven rules of thumb:

1. In tightly-scheduled parent and teacher conference days, use bells and insist on ending on time and scheduling another meeting if needed; backing up everyone else is inconsiderate and erodes confidence. Train teachers in how to end such a meeting in the face of a garrulous parent.
2. Six weeks before reports are written, make sure every teacher has conveyed to parents by phone or e-mail any current nega-

tives and has invited a follow-up discussion. *Allow no new neg-atives in written term-end reports.*

3. Similarly, *allow no diagnoses of learning or psychological issues in term-end reports.* These belong *only* in private conferences and can come *only* from qualified professionals.
4. Make sure that reports include an appraisal of actual course content and skills learned as well as approach and habits.
5. Be sure that reports demonstrate knowledge of and apprecia-tion for each child as a person.
6. Encourage teachers to get an administrator to read a draft of a report on an especially challenging or vexing child.
7. Always get qualified second pairs of eyes to read and assess every report for tone, typos, and grammatical correctness: The cost and time taken to do so may be burdensome, but the pain of individual or institutional embarrassment is usually worse.

Paying attention to all the nuances of institutional relations with par-ents is an essential facet of school success. Parents send their chil-dren to us by choice. It takes little imagination to consider the conse-quences of their choosing not to do so.

Ideas for Building Community

Princeton Friends School has had such a palpable a sense of com-munity that when families leave or their children graduate, it is often the parents who feel an enormous sense of loss. Therein lie elements from which to learn. Thirty-two years ago, the school started with only nineteen children so it was, in effect, a cooperative school, although not technically so. For many years, PFS held Labor Day work parties to get the place ready to open, and seventy-five people came, includ-ing alumni parents. Those early days have passed, but parents remain involved in almost every field trip, community service outreach, major assembly, and holiday and culminating curricular celebration. They continue to be a source of expertise in all sorts of ways from marketing to setting long-term IT strategy.

Examples of PFS community building include:

> At arrival time, a senior administrator shakes hands with students, parents and colleagues in the parking lot, and others are present in the lobby. Someone is also in the lobby at dismissal time. The idea is to model availability, solve glitches on the spot, and respond to upsets immediately.

> At dismissal time, parents are required to come into the schoolhouse to pick up their children which creates daily contact with their children's advisors. One byproduct of that policy is parents getting to know each other despite coming from thirty-plus zip codes. It also improves upon a slow-motion line of 100-plus idling cars.

> Most School Committee meetings (finance, personnel, and executive committees excepted) are open and parents are invited to become volunteer members.

> The school employs all the usual buddy family and new-family orientation procedures.

> The major annual school fundraiser is in fact a community builder. Affordable "Frolics" offered by people from all constituent groups are sold or auctioned off. They are events that bring people together to do everything from sampling beers and learning to use boomerangs to taking family bike rides and fishing trips, joining adult book discussion groups, and attending a cappella concerts.

> Parents with expertise that fits into the curriculum are occasionally asked to work with the children. At times, some are consulted on developing curriculum as well.

> Every Friday, the whole school attends Quaker meeting and sings together; parents are invited to join in, and many do.

> Some parents offer Arts Electives (see page 19).

> Every May, just before Memorial Day, families of first-eighth graders who so choose embark on a two-night, three-day camping and outdoor adventure trip, with parents responsible

for their own children and sometimes the children of non-attendees. It is an enormous and successful community builder and extremely meaningful for graduating parents.

Chapter 11

Safety

By now, all independent schools and their summer camps have sound emergency plans vetted by local emergency officials, school attorneys, and insurance companies. Doubtless, they also have thorough community safety policies including sections on sexual harassment and employee contacts with students outside of school. Less often considered in my experience are the myriad day-to-day opportunities for adults to get it wrong. Here be dragons.

A few examples are: Teachers or parents with children in their cars or vans who do not strictly follow traffic laws, and that includes not insisting on buckled seat belts, exceeding speed limits and texting; coaches who don't bother to bring all the emergency safety equipment to practice every day; teachers who don't bother to take a walkie-talkie out to recess coverage or the trip to the far end of campus; and adults who are not assiduous in bringing emergency medications each time they leave the heart of campus with a child. The worst near-miss story I have heard concerned a head crew coach at a boarding school who knew he was going to be late to practice on a cold New England lake in early April. He permitted his assistant to allow the students to launch the shells before he arrived, but the head coach had the only key to the boat with the outboard motor. That was the day one of the shells swamped, and students clung to their boat for over twenty minutes in 50-ish degree water before being rescued. Fortunately, no one died, but just imagine…

My personal antidote for anything resembling inattention to safety or reckless behavior with students came from an attorney in Providence who said, "Pete, just imagine yourself on the stand in a courtroom in front of a hostile lawyer: *Mr. Jaques, the clearly posted speed limit was 30 when the accident happened but you were going 45 with students in the car, and Miss Smith is now permanently crippled. How do you explain that?*" Insert yourself and any circumstance you can imagine into such a scenario, or insert one of your school's employees or authorized parent drivers and…well, you get the point. Make the point with your faculty and parents early and often, *and make it clear that imperfect adherence by faculty and staff is a firing offense.* There is nothing more important than personal safety, and it is the job of administrators to do everything they can to both assure it and minimize risk to the school.

Chapter 12

Carving Out a Middle School

It's safe to say that middle schoolers are polarizing. The vast majority of teachers I've met don't want to go near them, while a minority thinks they are the best—"love 'em or hate 'em" is a common description. Middle school kids are different than their older and younger siblings and have different cognitive, social, and physical needs and burgeoning senses of spirituality. They benefit when their schools are different too—that's what the middle school revolution of the 1970s was all about.

The typical PK-12 or 6-12 school setup is simple. Lower and upper schools have distinct needs. The PK- 4th or -5th grades are based in homerooms and students depart for specialty classes such as library, PE, Mandarin, and art. The high school is set up to crank students through departmental curricular silos, and those students typically get priority for the better teachers, newer- or better-equipped class-rooms, and preferred time slots in the schedule. The middle school too often gets what's left, including remnants of the less effective upper-school teachers who need a class or two to fill out their schedules, spe-cialty class times that fall randomly, and classroom spaces that are not the most appealing or that change daily. I understand high school departmental silos, SAT2s, and AP Exams because I've taught AP U.S. History, and my own children also had to prepare for college. I have worked in four PK-12 schools and one with 6th-12th grades, and their middle schools all had pretty much identical issues. As the head of middle school in three of them, I developed sharp elbows, swam upstream, and absolutely knew what being a minority was all about. Middle schools and/or middle schoolers need:

1. Schedule independence—i.e., sufficient control to permit rearranging classes on a regular and impromptu basis without affecting upper and lower school schedules or room assignments.

2. Lively faculty members who *prefer* to teach 11- to 14-year-olds; evict those who are resigned to doing their one or two periods daily in middle school purgatory.

3. Classroom and gathering spaces that for the most part keep middle schoolers separate from upper school students, whom middle schoolers try too hard to emulate.

4. Structured opportunities to work with lower-school students, which helps to burst the early adolescent bubbles of burgeoning hormones and American pop culture. Middle schoolers appreciate being looked to for responsibility while still having a foot in childhood.

5. Genuinely challenging academic coursework, especially for the able students who have reached Piaget's Stage of Formal Operations and are fully motivated to succeed.

6. Plenty of variety in the way things are taught—after all, the middle school revolution was about escaping a junior high school mindset—and opportunities for experiential learning via real-world simulations, movement, fresh voices, and off-campus learning.

7. Thematic and cross-departmental academic coordination to give students multiple portals into subject matter.

8. Consistent and varied programs designed to both expose and suppress the inherent developmental tendency to "make yourself right by making someone else wrong."

9. A health, drugs, alcohol and sexuality course that emphasizes what makes for healthy human relationships.

10. Regular exposure to current events to engage their rapidly expanding horizons. Middle schoolers are truly motivated by issues of justice. Getting out into the real world to learn or to serve really pays off.
11. Cross-discipline coordination so students are not juggling simultaneous major assignments. Many still need to go to bed pretty early and travel a long way to and from school.
12. A tone of school and disciplinary approach as described in Chapter 9—teachers and division heads should understand and persuade at first and not be afraid to draw clear boundaries when "enough is enough."
13. Opportunities to try out a lot of different kinds of skills and activities as discussed in Chapter 5.

The hardest to achieve of this baker's dozen is scheduling independence, and it is crucial to overall success. The Moses Brown team model described in Chapter 4 works really well. Once a middle school has secured scheduling independence for a chunk or two of each day, achieving the rest of this list becomes easier, and the inherent genius of committed teachers will be unleashed.

Chapter 13

What to Teach?

Independent schools have always had to decide what to teach. The world's schools present different ideas—e.g., Finnish short days of school vs. East Asian full days followed by hours of intense tutoring, or French middle school examinations that create absolute forks in the road of life vs. American access at all ages to next educational levels. *What* we teach is inextricably linked to *how* we teach it, and *toward what societal end.* When we look at our graduates at various ages, we see lives and occupations of almost infinite variety. Wise people remind us that we are teaching students for worlds that have not yet been invented. As the United States population has become increasingly diverse and U.S. income inequality has eroded net tuition income, our schools have had to adapt in ways unimagined a generation ago. In the face of such expanding breadth, the questions of curricular content and pedagogy are enormous. With all due respect to the thousands of fine educators with doctorates and vast experience in curricular design, I dare to weigh in.

As a student in mainstream schools in the 1940s and 1950s, what I was taught was straightforward and standard: the 3 R's, dead white male history, the three sciences, Latin, French, Spanish or German, and minor subjects that became major subjects in high school for students who were "slow," weren't "college material," or were genuinely arts-bound. Such simplicity was long gone by the mid-1970s, obviated by multiple factors including the civil rights movement, the 1960s anti-war counterculture and its demand for relevance, the growth of social history, women's lib, drugs, experiments with Open Classroom, New Math, Initial Teaching Alphabet and many others, television in all its remarkable evolutions, and frank sex ed. The 1980s and beyond brought overwhelming change via PCs and Macs, the Internet, the information age, vastly improved psych-ed evaluations, brain research, a keener understanding of learning styles, and smart phones and their equivalents that swept into lives and schools.

All of these spawned backlashes and counterrevolutions such as Back to Basics, the rise and decline of IQ testing and Advanced Placement, the ascendance of public school achievement testing, e.g., No Child Left Behind, Race to the Top, the Common Core. Many of those were intended to address the dreadful, downward spiraling impact of poverty on children, families, and schools. Home schooling and charter schools were both symptoms and solutions. But nationally there has been a growing concern that our children have irretrievably changed in their lack of respect for authority and their shrinking attention spans.

In his recent book, *The Collapse of Parenting*, Dr. Leonard Sax makes two relevant points: that American parents have ceded their traditional authority to their children; and that the global ranking of American education has fallen notably from first in the world 30 years ago to "being on the second screen" today—from #17 to #35 depending on the specific subject. He asserts that American schooling's decline in relation to other countries corresponds precisely to our national obsession for greater technology in schools and the increases in personal screen time. He backs up his opinion with evidence from a growing number of studies demonstrating, for example, that students' comprehension declines when reading from screens vs. pages and from screens with links vs. plain ones. We're all familiar with the landslide of anecdotes about addiction to our devices and the shift from face-to-face conversation to social media. Indeed, addiction to our mobile devices is so potent that people kill and maim one another while texting at highway speed, and teen suicide rates reveal just how isolating technology-driven lives have become. Common sense tells us these are all related.

Many independent schools trumpet being "one-to-one," i.e., issuing an iPad or the equivalent to each student. In this information age, we certainly need to graduate students who are technologically proficient, and I applaud the Girls Who Code movement as an example. Yet I agree with a lot of thoughtful teachers who believe that we must match the use of technology to stages of cognitive maturity. All kids know how to play on computers, but young children and early teens need coaching on how to use them productively. For example, one seasoned and energetic fifth grade teacher at a well-known one-to-one independent school had grave doubts about the extent to which he was expected to employ computers in lessons; observing his kids getting lost, he frequently reverted to pencil, paper, and class discussion and found his students happier and more productive. Princeton Friends School has always taken a similarly balanced approach, believing that youngsters through 3rd grade have physical as well as cognitive developmental needs best served by employing pencil and paper, introducing tech skills and limited network access only in 4th and 5th grades, and employing computers thereafter as needed, but not always. When working with 7th and 8th graders on full-bore research papers, my colleagues and I emphasized instruction first in chunking, then outlining, and finally revising text to achieve cogency; my constant (and annoying) watchword was "Downloading ≠ Learning." I absolutely believe that if we don't insist on such moderate steps, the seduction of roaming the Internet inevitably prevails over developing critical thinking skills. Those skills are built upon guided discussions with teachers and among peers.

Three studies with overlapping results inform my concept of the overarching purposes of our schools. The first is the work of Douglas Heath that I described in Chapter 2. The second study was launched in Great Britain in 1946 and continues today. Its purpose was to identify what determines good lives for children and adults. Its 70,000 subjects were followed continuously throughout their lives. (*ted.com Helen Pearson|TED2017 Lessons from the longest study on human development*) Their primary factors for achieving positive lives were, in order of priority: (1) whether or not children grew up in poverty, and (2) fifteen minutes of daily time reserved for parent–child conversation and regular bedtime routines including reading books aloud. A third study, the Harvard Study of Adult Development that was launched in 1930, is similar. It originated with two groups, that year's Harvard sophomore class and an equal-sized group of older teenaged boys who grew up in limited circumstances in Boston. The original group of 724 was personally and extensively surveyed every two years. As young men, many sought high achievement, fame, and wealth, and some succeeded while others did not. In the end, however, what supported happy, healthy lives were none of those three; instead, the quality of their human relationships emerged as the key. Loneliness, even among the most successful of people, was proven to have a corrosive effect on the duration and quality of lives. The original study has been renewed with new subjects of both genders and is now on its fourth director. (*ted.com Robert Waldinger TEDxBeaconStreet What makes a good life Lessons from the longest study on happiness*)

Furthermore, a credible former colleague told me about two surveys for which I can locate no sources to cite. The first was conducted in the mid-1960s; the second was a repeat 30 years later. They sought to determine what factors National Merit Scholarship winners had in common and listed multiple possibilities from which to choose. In both cases, only one predominant commonality emerged: the families of top scholars ate dinner together most every night, and the students benefitted from regular intergenerational conversations.

Over my five-decade career, computers and their spawn have been by far the greatest agents of change. At the same time, however, we also know and bemoan the darker, addictive side of our technologies. The overwhelming message of the five studies described above is that promoting the development and sustenance of meaningful interpersonal skills and strong human relationships is something we should prioritize as we build curricula and the school structures that support them.

As for the material we teach in schools, I am a firm believer in two old-fashioned objectives: (1) the 3 Rs, updated of course, and (2) cultural literacy.

> The updated 3 Rs mean drilling in grammar, vocabulary, reading for content, math facts, science and tech competence, writing cogently, speaking to groups and logical argument. Children need to do the calisthenics required to be competent as they move through both school and life. (Some newer software provides tools to do this in more varied and interesting ways than in the past.) There's no substitute for these basics, and people can be limited for life without them. I have *not* interviewed and *not* hired adults who clearly lacked such knowledge or skills, and am aware of too many reports from industrial leaders who decry the national dearth of candidates qualified to fill jobs requiring such competence.

> Cultural literacy, also the title of a 1987 book by Professor E.D. Hirsch Jr., means being conversant with the basics of geography, American history, governance, sociology, economic factors, inequities, and seminal individuals. While the 5,000-item list of suggested knowledge at the end of Hirsch's book is controversial, I absolutely support his overriding thesis. Here's an illustrative but mortifying, story: At Princeton Friends School, social studies was once taught only employing overarching annual themes, e.g., Walls and Bridges, Cultural Chemistry, and Among Trees. A PFS family took a trip to Washington, DC, and as they moved down the National Mall to the Lincoln Memorial, their 4th-grade daughter asked aloud and in public, "Who's the big guy in the chair?" Unfortunately she was wearing a Princeton Friends School shirt. Needless to say, her parents were embarrassed, and the school began adding more formal history instruction not long thereafter.

As a social studies and history teacher, I am continually amazed and saddened by the number of adults who discover an interest in history after having been bored to tears as students. Now an avid birder and an eager if only aspiring naturalist, I once hated science in the same way. Ditto for my career in French. Boring teaching and vast quantities of rote learning were the two major perpetrators.

Rigor vs. *Vigor*: The juxtaposition of these two words came from Dr. Irene McHenry, longtime teacher, founding head of two Friends schools, psychologist, educational thinker, and acclaimed former Executive Director of the Friends Council on Education.

➢ *Rigor* is one of those words that appears on most schools' websites and in most publications, implying that a school *really* challenges students intellectually. I certainly acknowledge the worth of rigorous academic training, but revolt when *rigor* grows legs of its own. It is so easy for teachers to pile work on students no matter how well considered each assignment might be. But is there truly value in that? "Play is the work of children," said no less an educator than Maria Montessori, and others have added, "and they are 100% employed." The younger the students, the more free time matters to their development. A few years ago, a most reasonable parent let us know how sad she was when her 4th grader informed her that he was too busy to go with the family on a weekend activity that he loved. The reason was too much homework. Egads! Parents losing family time due to their work is a nationally recognized problem, but 4th graders? Calls for no homework go too far, but *Race to Nowhere,* the film about the unremitting pressure schools put on more capable, ambitious teenagers, probably has it about right: Everyone needs time to tune out, play a little, recharge, and be with family and friends. Upon reflection, it certainly was blind adherence to rigor that made much of my own education so very dull.

➢ *Vigor*, on the other hand, has some marvelous synonyms—dynamism, activity, liveliness— and some depressing antonyms—dullness, inertia, lifelessness. The latter typified my aforementioned education in history, science, and French. The former are what clearly have most motivated my students over the years. The broad acceptance in the past decade of project- and inquiry-based education is exciting and makes common sense on multiple levels. Such lessons are often minds-on *and*

64

hands-on, which is widely recognized as a better way to learn for most people. They allow students to follow their own interests, always a motivator; they get kids out of their seats, using their hands as well as their heads; they promote peer teaching and appreciation and promote collaboration and compromise; and they enhance students' presentation skills.

Jane Fremon and Nancy Wilson, co-founders of Princeton Friends School, attracted Dr. Ernest Boyer to the launching of that new school in 1987, so much so that he agreed to serve on the school's original Advisory Committee. Dr. Boyer, one of the most important thinkers in American education, said, "Education must prepare students to be independent, self-reliant human beings. But education, at its best, also must help students go beyond their private interests, gain a more integrative view of knowledge, and relate their learning to the realities of life." (Ernest L. Boyer 1997). He also said, "Our most consequential human problems will be resolved, not through competition, but collaboration. And what we need in education is a learning climate in which students work together. In such an atmosphere, truth emerges as authentic insights are conscientiously exchanged." ("Ernest L. Boyer, Selected Speeches, 1979-1995," Jossey-Bass)

My most successful moments as a teacher of history and social studies mirrored Dr. Boyer's thinking. I have found that almost nothing resonates more with students of all ages than issues of fairness and justice. Creating scenarios built around such issues, giving students adult roles to play, having the roles be naturally conflicting, and requiring students to research and prove knowledge of the positions their characters would support in a debate were preliminary steps that prepared them for two to three full days in character in mock citizens' conferences that strictly followed Robert's Rules of Order. Examples of subject matter included debating the routing of a proposed second Alaska pipeline, arguing whether or not to support British taxation of Americans in the 1760s, and choosing to support or oppose the building of a big dam across the Nu-Salween River in China. Another type of successful activity came from the invention of school-wide outdoor games that required commercial trading. One involved Amazonian rainforest products, another diverse resources from a variety of ancient Mediterranean nation-states. Each game had plenty of rules and structures to pose group dilemmas. We also utilized a pair of high-quality simulations about Ellis Island and the Silk Road. Judging from their subsequent reflections on learning, such activities absolutely elevated the students' levels of engagement. While such exercises simulate real-world experiences in meaningful ways, Miss Hall's School goes one better with its Horizons program. Every Thursday morning, all students take part in formal, year-long programs that start with on-campus service and research work in 9th grade and expand to individually planned internships in junior and senior years, with those girls leaving campus to work in some 75 business, medical, arts, governmental, environmental, educational, and other settings locally and in surrounding towns and counties.

Throughout my career, brilliant colleagues have created curricula that have generated equivalent enthusiasm in Spanish, science, music, drama, mathematics, art, writing, and more. It is striking to see kids—even in primary-grades—come to life and to watch their capabilities emerge when we give them real world problems to solve that require balancing individual and group needs along with crisp thinking, listening, clear expression, and persuasion. Taking the time to work through issues in discussion allows such skill building to happen. Quaker schools are especially good at this.

In summary, I believe:

➤ Schools would not exist without academics at their heart.
➤ The updated 3 Rs and cultural literacy are crucial for students and for the sustenance of the American republic.
➤ Rigor has its place but has been the source of two significant negatives—wearing out young people and encouraging dull teaching.
➤ Technology has its place but is a beast to be harnessed, a tool to be used only as needed.
➤ Children are most engaged when they are following their own interests, learning by doing, collaborating, working within struc-

tured discourse, and exposed frequently to the broader world and real work of adults.

➤ In addition to being trained for the next educational level, students are people who must enter the adult world *already* firmly grounded in successful interpersonal skills. Strong human relationships have been proven to make the primary difference between having good lives and bad ones long after we, their teachers, are gone.

Chapter 14

Nourishing School Heads and Trustees

Having been a nonprofit trustee for 35 years, having worked extremely closely with eight school heads over four decades and been an acting head of school for two more, I know firsthand that school heads need plenty of reinforcement to be their best. Teachers and operational staff are widely recognized as the people who make schools resonate for student and parents. Yet it is trustees and heads of school who have authority and whose decisions have schoolwide impacts. Really good heads won't join schools with ineffective, interfering, petty boards, or won't long remain, and really good heads are key to empowering faculty and staff talents. Similarly, it is the relative strength of board-head relationships that allow heads and their schools to flourish. Consequently, those who work in independent schools can have significant impacts by supporting both.

The headship of an independent school is a massive job as well as an inspiring one. Multiply a school's enrollment by three, add all the employees, some grandparents, significant donors and friends of the school, trustees and a healthy number of graduates, and that sum will be the number of people who believe they ought to have prompt access to the head. Furthermore, a responsible head's total workweek typically starts at about seventy-five hours and jumps incrementally with every significant crisis. Heads are expected to be available to all, simultaneously familiar with everything from fire door code to best Mandarin instructional practices and current national educational trends, fully knowledgeable about finances, and be prescient in peering over the horizon. They must have the poise of George Washington, the wisdom of Maya Angelou, the expressive ability of Obama, the stamina of a Kenyan marathoner, and the patience of a spider. Of necessity, heads harbor secrets and grave concerns, which makes for some professional loneliness. And, lest we forget, they themselves are spouses and parents.

To best support heads of school, it is necessary to understand and respect all of that. Let them know what they need to know. Never set them up to be surprised. Tell them when they're doing a good job and about your own successes—they frequently confront only problems. Express concerns privately. Give them time to consider. Give them credit when it's due, and urge colleagues to do the same. Well-nourished heads carry whole schools and communities forward.

Accepting an independent school trusteeship is a considerable volunteer commitment as well as an entrée to truly rewarding community service. It's an opportunity to fully support an organization, a mission, an idea, and a community that resonates deeply. It's also a promise to show up, learn the multiple sides of many issues, be very discreet, give and ask for money and other kinds of support, be an ambassador, work as part of a group in which your ideas may not prevail, and never cross the line between governance and management. All schools encounter big storms; well-trained and thoughtfully led boards are the sand dunes and salt marshes that absorb them. Marvelous golden ages in the lives of schools are the result of pairing steady, sturdy boards with strong, secure heads of school.

Most trustees lack operational school experience, yet they need to know how to guide both an institution and their sole employee, the school's head. Only well-informed board members can fully understand both the operation and culture of a school, and classic board-head conflicts can occur when trustees don't. Thus, it's often helpful and confidence-building for trustees to hear presentations and anecdotes from people other than the head and the finance professionals. As ambassadors and cheerleaders they need stories to tell so periodic encounters with students and teachers are valuable. Trustees should beware of gossip and *never* bring personnel matters to the board; those are the province of the head. In short, to be a trustee is to make a real commitment of time, open-mindedness, and personal funds. Excellent trustees are true treasures and all of us should appreciate and support them.

Chapter 15

Upon Further Reflection

Five years ago, I was on a community service trip, raking leaves and litter at a local no-budget nonprofit. A new 4th-grade girl and I—our backgrounds and ages couldn't have been more different—were working on the same pile, and I was griping about people who toss their trash. We talked for a while about how one learns not to do that, but then she turned the tables on me and calmly and thoughtfully said, "But if you think about it, Pete, if you know someone is going to pick up after you, why not litter?" My automatic reaction was negative, but I couldn't overcome her logic. We agreed that I'd think about it, and I have. This past June, that same slight, frank girl gave a remarkably calm, thoughtful, and honest 8th-grade graduation speech. It took me some time but I came to recognize that she has always been my better at speaking truth gently and bravely. It has been a relief to learn to accept wisdom from a child.

Recently, I happened to encounter a former student who was finishing up NYU Law School. He reminded me of a chance anecdote I'd related a decade prior in his 6th-grade social studies class: Back in the late 1950s, a Marblehead, Massachusetts town meeting motion to fund an ambulance was defeated by one vote. The next day, I overheard two of my parents' friends openly and unhappily admit that they hadn't bothered to attend the meeting because they'd assumed the motion would pass easily. Their brief story stayed with me and somehow led to my retelling it in a lesson on democracy 50 years later. That, in turn, had struck a chord with my former student, a future history major and now an attorney, who reminded me of that class ten years ago. Amazing. We can never know what is going to fully resonate.

At my 50th Middlesex School reunion, I met my former football coach and housemaster, Ted Childs, who was one of my favorite teachers. Fifty-one years prior, he'd spent an hour or two with me as I eagerly showed him a few football plays I'd drawn up. He even had the grace to put one into a game plan. I was able to tell him how much his brief generosity shaped my life, as I had happily gone on to coach middle and high school football for a couple of decades. My pleasure in thanking him face-to-face was too soon joined by deep regret for not having reached out to him sooner, nor to so many others now lost or dead.

We who work honestly with young people can be stunned decades later by what they tell us of impacts we never knew we'd had. Such revelations remind me that we who lead in schools have a profound obligation to enable our colleagues and charges to flourish so that they, too, can pay it forward.

Acknowledgments

Tom Shepard, my late father-in-law, was an exemplar of Tom Brokaw's "Greatest Generation." A riches-to-rags-to-riches product of the Great Depression and World War II and the publisher of *LOOK* magazine, Tom was thoroughly tuned into the world and always aware of poignant moments. It was he who, upon hearing of my early mornings in the parking lot at Princeton Friends School, titled this book before it was begun.

As Sean Compagnucci wrote in his acknowledgments for the Friends Council on Education's *Advices and Queries*, "If ever there were a co-authored document, this is it." I cannot improve on that description. So much of my professional learning came directly from the wisdom of hundreds of my profoundly inspired, ethical, talented, tough, caring, professional, and diligent colleagues. In my text, I mention some individuals who shaped my professional growth at specific times, but I do not attempt to name many others who have been my betters and with and from whom I learned what I know. Although I usually occupied the higher chair, it was I who so often sat in awe at their feet.

George Fox created Quakerism in the 1600s. He taught that there is "that of God" in everyone, and that people could have their own direct relationships with God. Since Quaker worship is silent until a Friend is moved to speak, every voice is heard equally, and that equality is central to the respect with which Friends schools and their graduates are widely held. Quakers have informed a great deal of my practice as teacher, colleague, and leader, and for that I am grateful.

Peter Mott, my former Middlesex School teacher and housemaster and later Head of Moses Brown School, showed me how inspirational true support of one's colleagues could be. Jane Fremon and Nancy Wilson, with whom I began working at Princeton Day School and who co-founded Princeton Friends School, are brilliant teachers and visionaries who taught me endlessly. At the latter school, I was frequently inspired by two more remarkable scholars and highly accomplished professionals, Richard Fischer and Shu Shu Costa.

My children Buck, Charlie, Tim, and Thayer, and stepsons, Mac and Rocky, endured life as faculty brats, had a father or stepfather who worked too many hours for too little money, bravely coped with friends who were disciplined by my hand, and occasionally had to keep secrets that no other kids did. They somehow managed all of that and more with generosity and grace.

My brother, Bill Jaques, who in his five-decade career provided outstanding governance and fundraising guidance to hundreds of nonprofits great and small, supplied me with regular and crucial doses of knowhow, wise counsel, and humor.

Sue Shepard Jaques, my wife and life partner of 38 years, has enriched me with her keen mind, uncommon and independent perspective, courageous frankness, fine editing, remarkable support, and great a cappella. She has guided and carried me through many a crucible, and it's been a thrill to be her roadie and best pal.